PHOTOPLAY!

Doodle · Design · Draw.

by m·j· bronstein

chronicle books · san francisco

WELCOME!

Would you design an outfit for me? Don't forget to give me a camera and a pair of cool boots, please.

My name is Marcie. I'm a professional photographer, an art educator at the Center for Maine Contemporary Art, and the creator of this book. As you'll soon see, it's filled with photographs. Here's why:

As a young child I loved art. But I especially loved photography. Looking through the lens of my camera, seeing the world close-up, was fascinating. I felt like an explorer on a treasure hunt, where there was *always* treasure to be found.

Through the years, traveling the world and taking thousands of photographs, I've met many marvelous friends. In just a moment, you'll meet them, too.

So I truly love photographs. But this is not the end of my story. I'm also crazy about drawings. Many years ago, I combined my photographs with some drawings and guess what happened? *PhotoPlay!*

To learn more about me and to see examples of completed *PhotoPlay!* pages, visit www.inthisplayground.com.

WHAT MIGHT YOU DO WITH THIS BOOK?

Draw right on top of the photographs? Yes!

Design something that seems goofy or impossible? Yes!

Color outside of the lines? Yes!

Laugh out loud at my photographs? Yes!

Laugh out loud at your drawings? Why not?!

With your pencils, crayons, markers, and your wide-open imagination, it's your turn to step, jump, run, or dive right in!

Grace and Ian are leaping into a wild and wondrous world . . .

Victor is swimming near a long, graceful sea monster.

Yikes! Jaco's swing needs to hang from something. Design it!

What has Eliza discovered?

An underwater garden? A magnificent palace? Another universe?

Something is jumping out of the water!
Will Ian catch it?

Sarah doesn't see what
Suzette and Sam see.

Carson loves to dive.
Draw the rest of his body.

What's swimming in this pool?

Alex and Coffee are a great team.

They're remembering their most dazzling, daring jump . . .

Linda is waiting for her rider and her saddle. She wants to jump, too!

This is Zelda. She's not only a zebra, she's a spider.
Draw her zebra-spider body.

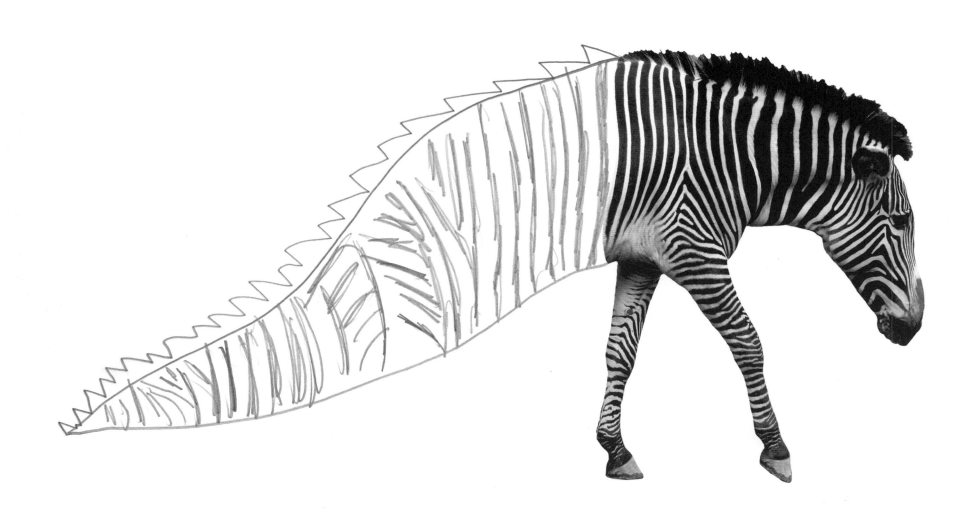

Which adorable creatures are following Zelda?

What's inside of
Jake's camera?

Gracie loves to gaze at her garden in the spring.

Sasha and Gail like to balance small objects on their heads.

What does Ariel like to balance?

Zane stepped into a fairy tale to visit his friend Freddie.

Create their magical setting . . .

Freddie is meeting his long lost friend Freda. What happens when they kiss?

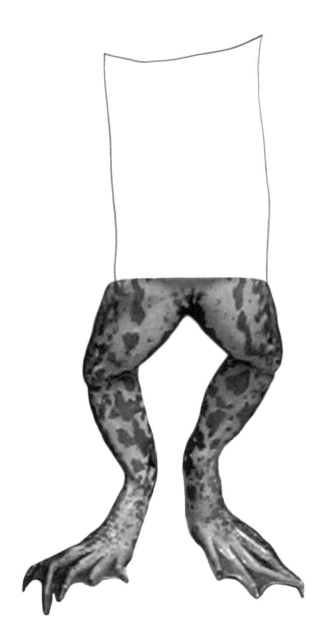

Is Freddie half frog and half prince?

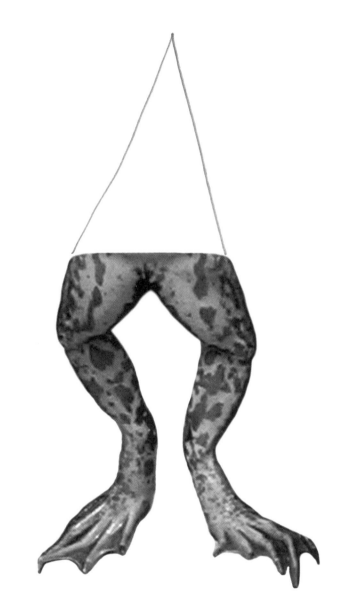

Is Freda half frog and half princess?

Draw the other half of Bruce's face. Fill the background with a sunrise.

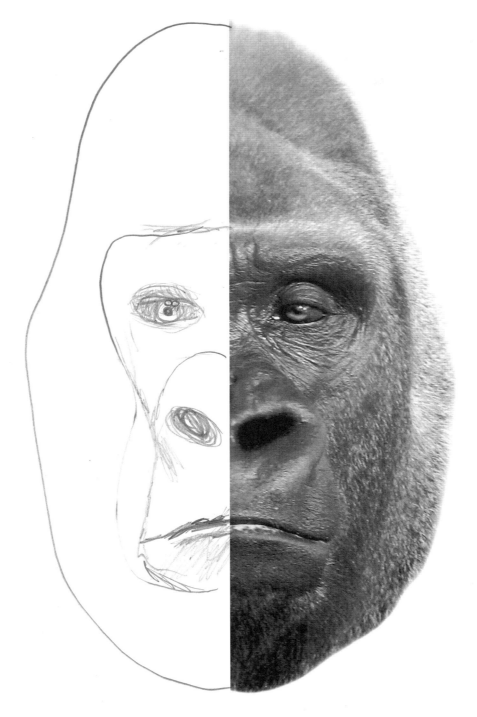

Draw the other half of Gregory's face. Fill the background with a sunset.

Draw David's twin.

Draw Leah's father.

Schnibbles is in his favorite class in school.
Who is his teacher?

Marcie would like to go to school to learn to fly.

It's Bob's birthday, and he's walking in to his party!

Draw a tasty cake for Bob.

Barbara, Barry, Jane, and Will are looking at a fantastic feathered creature.

Jesse and Puffy are watching an alien.

Marcie is watching an alien, too.
This one wears fabulous shoes.

Things look so different when you're upside down!

Try it yourself . . . then draw something that looks sooooo different.

Stefano is in his favorite seat. Draw the rest of his house.

This is your house. And that's you in the window!

Bebe, Pepper, and Hugh are watching a parade.

People you love are looking out at you . . .

Eleanor is speaking with her elegant friend Edward.

There's so much to see on a safari!

Gregory is on the lookout.
He's protecting something important.

Daniel is on the lookout, too . . . for what?

Grace is taking a walk with her pet.

This mucky puddle is no place for J.T.,
the most stylish pet in town.

There's something strange on the horizon . . .

. . . and on the beach, too.

Jeremiah sees something amazing.

Maya wants to catch it.

What might you find when you dig deep down in the sand?

Dinosaur bones? A chest filled with jewels? A passage into another country?

Noah and Elizabeth found buried treasure.

What kind of treasure is in that window?

This is a passage that leads
to your favorite place in the world.

This
tunnel is
overflowing
with . . .

What a lovely village. Who lives here? Is there a playground or a swimming pool?

Someone's having fun.

And someone's about to score.

Java is bored.
Draw him some toys to play with.

Cleo and Chloe are not bored. What are they playing with?

Your friend is giving you what you've always wanted.

Jaco is playing hide-and-seek.
Where are his friends hiding?

Ravi is waving to his imaginary friend, Ryan.

Your imaginary friend is
inviting you into a secret fort.

Meet your new friends!

What are their names?

Could this be you?

Dylan is on a road trip to see the bright colors of autumn.

Imagine if pigeon feathers
were like autumn leaves.
What colors might they be?

Dylan loves watching the boats on the bay.

Alan is trying to take an afternoon nap. He needs a cozy couch.

There's something heavy on this sled.

Dylan sees a snow monster.

Elizabeth and her friends are learning to skate. Who else has joined them?

What would you like to learn to do?
Draw it . . . and it may come true!

There's simply no way
Kristin and Chris will go outside today.

What wild weather!

Patrisha found the most unexpected place to perch.

Carol and Bill are leaving. Where have they been?

Harold and his family are flying south for the winter.
Is it sunny . . . or stormy?

Look! There's a rainbow!

Lindsay is not so sure she wants to eat that!

This is what
Lindsay wants to eat!

Emma is looking for the perfect place to build a nest.

These chairs are perfect. For whom?

Carly just woke from a crazy dream!

The world is such a
mysterious place . . .

This passage leads to your worst nightmare . . .

. . . and this leads to your most wonderful dream.

This is your castle . . .

The queen has turned into stone! She's so sad. What happened?

Ralph turned into stone, too! His shield wasn't able to protect him. From what?

There are zombies in this house.

Is that a zombie on the hill? Maybe it's a friendly zombie.

What's making
all that noise?

Create a story that begins with a whisper.

This house was abandoned a long time ago. Rebuild it!

They're having a serious conversation about their seriously silly hats.

This is your new store.
It needs a name.
What will you sell?

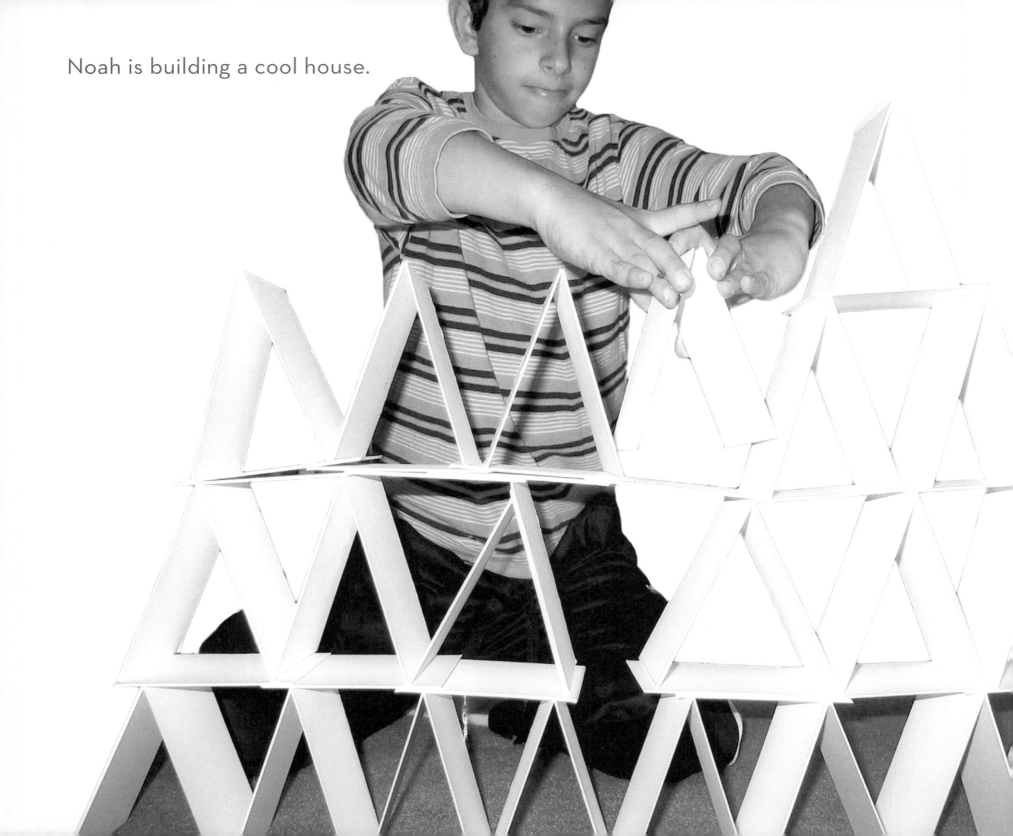

Noah is building a cool house.

What can you add to make it even cooler?

Fill these vases with flowers
from another planet.

Design an unusual vase.

Make some beautiful art for these walls.

Look! People are coming to see your work!

Help Joanne design a robot.

Draw some fantastical fish to swim beneath this fantastic bridge.

There's a bright city on the horizon.

Ari, Sophie, and Dylan
think it's beautiful here.

Liz thinks you've
done some fine work!
Draw a picture of yourself.

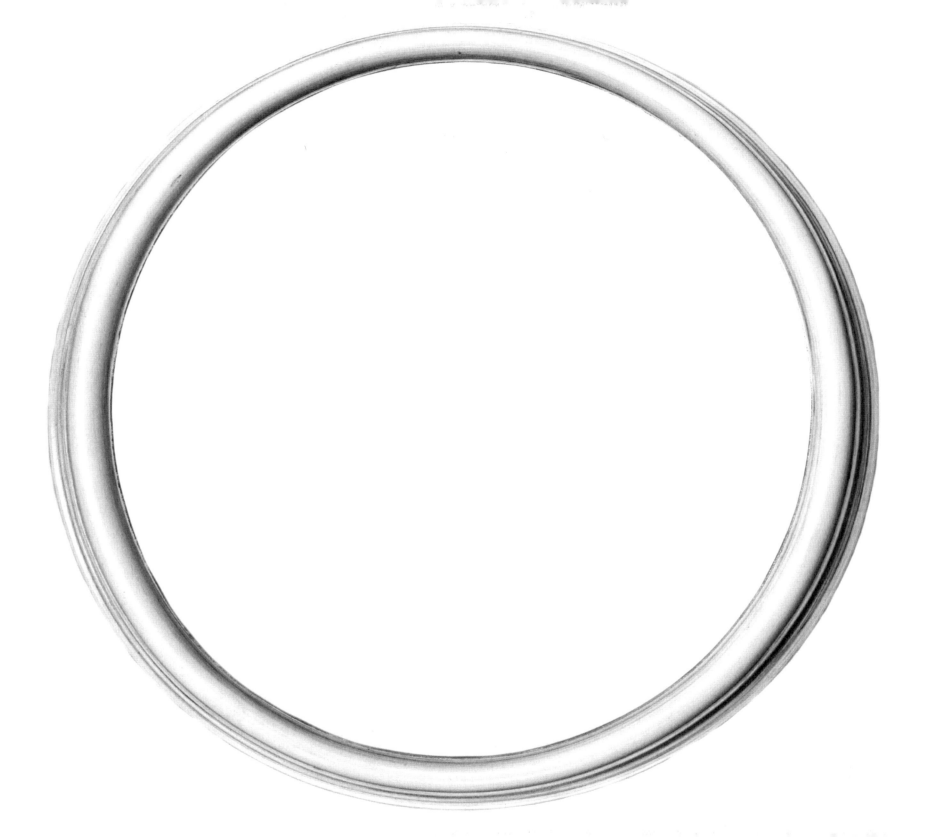

*For Linda Stec, Rebecca Childs,
and the children at the Starrett
Children's Center in Belfast, Maine*

-----------and-----------

*for Tonia Bochińska, Joanna Zarańska,
and the children of the Early Stage
School in Warsaw, Poland.*

Credits:
Back cover: owl by Noah Fishman.
Page 3: zebra-unicorn by Isabel Refford;
alien in the window by Noah Fishman;
frog-guy by Nicholas Flagg.

ISBN 978-1-4521-2341-7

Manufactured in China.

MIX
Paper from
responsible sources
FSC® C008047

Design by Ryan Hayes.
Typeset in Neutra.

10 9 8 7 6 5 4 3 2 1

Chronicle Books LLC
680 Second Street
San Francisco, CA 94107

Chronicle Books—we see things differently. Become part of our
community at www.chroniclekids.com.